Go Wild
BE AN EXPLORER

Thanks to the creative team:

Senior Editor: Alice Peebles

Designer: Lauren Woods and
collaborate agency

First published in Great Britain in 2015
by Hungry Tomato Ltd

PO Box 181

Edenbridge

Kent, TN8 9DP

Copyright © 2015 Hungry Tomato Ltd

A CIP catalogue record for this book is available
from the British Library.

ISBN 978-1-910684-14-6

Printed and bound in China

Discover more at
www.hungrytomato.com

Go Wild

BE AN EXPLORER

by Chris Oxlade

Illustrated by Eva Sassin

HUNGRY
TOMATO™

CONTENTS

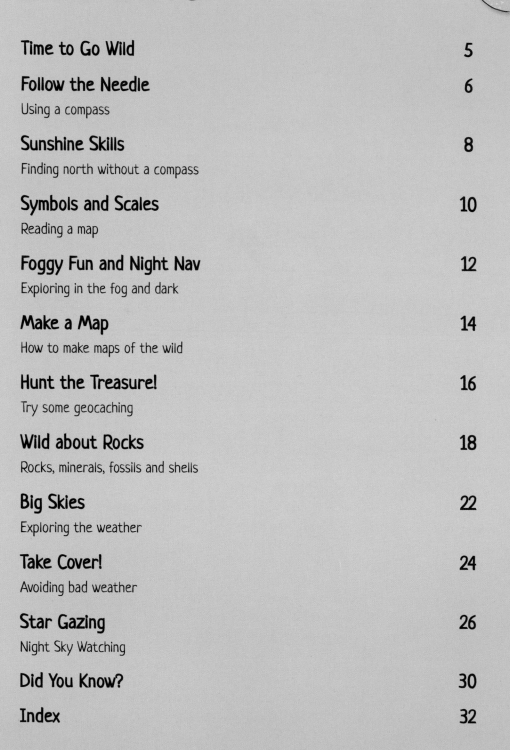

TIME TO GO WILD

Where do you go to have fun? Have you tried exploring the great outdoors? No? Then it's time to go wild! Out in the wild you can go exploring, see amazing natural sights and have loads of fun. So how about putting down your tablet, switching off your games console, stepping out of the door and trying some of the great activities in this book. Even if you live in the middle of the city, you can have a wild time in your garden or your local park.

In Go Wild – Be an Explorer, discover some of the skills you'll need for exploring in the wild, and find interesting stuff to look at on the ground and in the sky – without getting lost or caught out by the weather.

WILD SAFETY

• Never go exploring in the wild without an adult.

• Ask an adult before you do any of the projects in this book. In particular, ask before going near or in water, going to the coast, exploring in bad weather or in the dark, and using a GPS.

CARING FOR THE ENVIRONMENT

Always take care of the environment when you are in the wild. That means:

• Never damage rocks, animals or plants.

• Take special care to keep fires under control, and make sure a fire is out before you leave it.

FOLLOW THE NEEDLE

USING A COMPASS

A compass is your most important tool for exploring in the wild. A compass needle always points to magnetic north, so you can use a compass to check which direction you are moving in. Without a compass you might end up walking in circles!

Digital compass

Orienteering compass

Button compass with plate

Lost...

COMPASS POINTS AND DEGREES

A compass rose shows the four main directions: north, east, south and west.

The red end of the needle always points north. An orienteering compass also shows the direction in degrees, as shown in the picture.

Following a compass

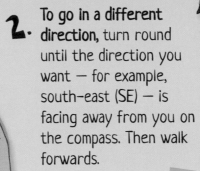

1. **Using a button compass with a plate:** hold the compass in the palm of your hand and let the plate settle. The N arrow will point north. To walk north, turn yourself until the N is pointing directly away from you. Now you can walk forwards.

2. **To go in a different direction,** turn round until the direction you want — for example, south-east (SE) — is facing away from you on the compass. Then walk forwards.

3. **Using an orienteering compass:** turn the dial until the direction you want lines up with the red arrow on the baseplate. Hold the compass flat and turn around until the red arrow lines up with the lines on the base plate. Then walk forwards.

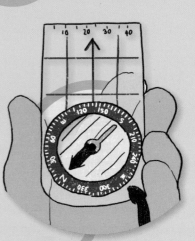

Make your own compass

If you lose your compass, you can make one with a needle and magnet.

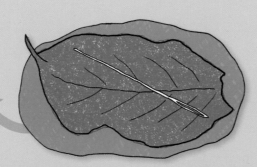

1. Find a needle and stroke it towards the point with the north end of a bar magnet (labelled N and normally coloured red). Lift the magnet away. Repeat this about twenty times. This will magnetize the needle.

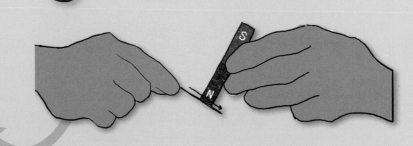

2. Place the needle on a dry leaf in a dish of water or in a puddle.

3. The leaf will slowly turn until the tip of the needle points north.

SUNSHINE SKILLS

FINDING NORTH WITHOUT A COMPASS

What if you are in the wild without a compass? You can find true north by measuring the position of the Sun, and by looking for clues in the landscape.

Checking shadows

On a sunny day you can find north with just a stick!

1. Find or make a stick about 1.2 metres long, and push it a little way into the ground, making sure it's as vertical as you can get it. Mark the ground at the end of the stick's shadow with a stone.

2. Wait at least 15 minutes, then put another stone at the end of the shadow. Place another stick in line with the stones. This stick will be lined up east to west. In the northern hemisphere, north is perpendicular to it, facing away from the shadow. In the southern hemisphere, it is the other way, facing towards the shadow.

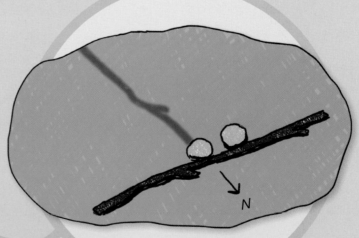

Using a watch

For this, you need a watch with hands, not a digital watch.

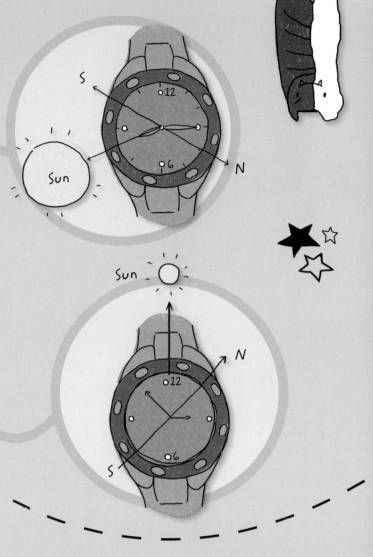

1. In the northern hemisphere, turn the watch until the hour hand points directly at the Sun. Now imagine a line halfway between the 12 on the watch face and the hour hand. That line points south, so north is the opposite way.

2. In the southern hemisphere, point the 12 on the watch face at the Sun; north is halfway between the 12 and the hour hand.

Looking at nature

If you have neither a compass nor watch, don't panic! Look for other clues to help you find north.

1. In the northern hemisphere, moss tends to grow thicker and greener on the north side of trees and walls, which are normally in shadow. In the southern hemisphere, it's the other way round.

2. In winter in the northern hemisphere, snow melts faster on the south-facing side of walls and hills, so the snowier side faces north. It's the other way round in the southern hemisphere.

The right-hand side of this tree faces north.

Help! I'm melting!

SYMBOLS AND SCALES

READING A MAP

Maps contain loads of information about the wild places around you. They show roads and paths, rivers, hills and valleys, forests, buildings and so on. So it's handy to get some map-reading skills before going exploring.

Looking at map symbols

For this project, you need a map of your local area, where you live.

—— Park boundary	●● Footpath
∞ walls	> Uphill path
—— Hedges and fences	▶ Access point
▭ Trees	◯ Pond
⚡ View point	⌒ Picnic Area
P Car park	≫ Steep uphill path
▭ Residential area / building	

1. Look for the key on your map. It shows what the symbols on the map mean.

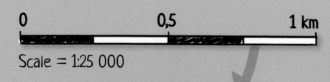

0   0,5   1 km

Scale = 1:25 000

2. Look for the scale on your map. This shows what a distance on the map equals in the real world. For example, on a town map, 1 centimetre on the map might be equal to 100 metres on the ground, a scale of 1 : 10,000, whereas in the above scale 1 centimetre represents 250 metres.

3. Try some measuring on your map. Find two places on the map (such as your house and school, or your house and the railway station). Put the edge of a piece of paper between the two places and mark both places on the paper.

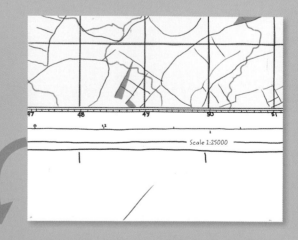

4. Now put the paper on the scale, with one mark at zero, and read off the distance.

Orientating a map

To orientate a map, you line up the map with the ground, so that things on the map match the things on the ground. You can do this by eye.

1. Stand where you can get a good view, such as on a hilltop, and then find that place on your map.

2. Search the map for landmarks, such as tall buildings, rivers and roads, and try to find them on the landscape. Hold the map flat and turn it so that it matches the landscape.

3. All maps have north at the top, so you can orientate the map with a compass, too. Hold the map flat and put your compass on top. Turn the map until the compass needle points to the top of the map.

Important note: compasses point to magnetic north, which isn't always exactly the same as 'true' north on a map. Where you live there may be quite a difference between the two.

(!)

FOGGY FUN AND NIGHT NAV

EXPLORING IN THE FOG AND DARK

It's sometimes cloudy or foggy in the wild! And at night it's dark. This makes it hard to see landmarks, and you can even get lost when you think you know where you're going. You might end up walking round in circles!

SAFETY IN THE FOG

Always take an adult with you when you go exploring in the wild, especially when it's foggy or dark.

Finding the way in fog

Here's how you stop yourself from going in circles in the fog. Don't try this in dangerous terrain — for example, where there are steep drops. You can practise these skills when it's not foggy!

1. Decide which direction you want to go in, then set your compass so that you are facing in that direction. Now send a friend straight ahead, shouting 'go left' or 'go right' to keep him or her on the right line.

2. Shout 'stop' just before he or she disappears into the fog. Now catch up with your friend.

3. Start over again, so that you go in a straight line in a series of steps. You can try the same project at night, using torches to see each other.

12

Searching for a landmark

If you are lost in the fog or the dark, try an organised search to find a landmark.

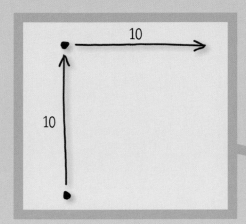

1. First try a 'spiral' search. You need a compass for this. Walk 10 double paces north, then turn right, and walk 10 double paces east.

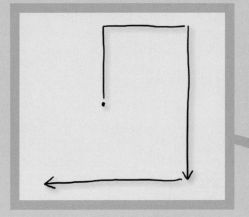

2. Turn right again and walk 20 double paces south. Turn right again and walk 20 double paces west.

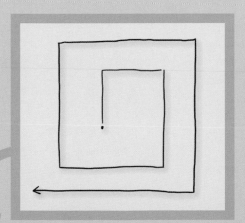

3. Repeat steps 1 and 2. After every two legs, increase the distance you walk by 10 double paces, so that would be 30 north, 30 east, 40 south, 40 west, and so on.

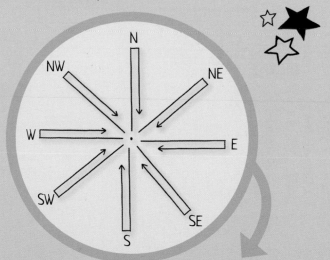

4. Now try a radial search pattern. Mark your position somehow. You could put a stick in the ground, or build a small pile of stones. Walk 20 double paces away to the north, turn and walk back south (in the opposite direction) until you find the mark you made. Now walk to the north-east, then to the east, and so on.

MAKE A MAP

HOW TO MAKE MAPS OF THE WILD

The brave people who explored the world hundreds of years ago had no maps. They had to make their own. Try making your own map of the place you are exploring, which might be a desert island or your local park.

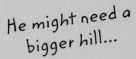

He might need a bigger hill...

Measuring how far you walk

To make a map, you need to measure how far one landmark is from another. Do this simply by pacing: counting how many steps it takes to walk between the two places.

80 paces = 100 metres
60 seconds = 100 metres

1. Measure your paces first. Mark out a distance of 50 metres along a straight path, using a tape measure or a length of string to mark every metre. Walk the 50 metres at a steady speed, counting how many double paces it takes, (count one every time your right foot hits the ground). Also time how long it takes to walk the 50 metres.

2. Multiply by two to find out how many paces or seconds it takes you to walk 100 metres. Write your answers down on a piece of paper. Now you can use these numbers to measure distance.

Make a map on the ground

Practise your mapping skills by making a map of a campsite or local park, using sticks and leaves to draw the map.

1. Clear a space on the ground for your map. Start mapping at a landmark, such as your camp, and make a simple shape to represent it.

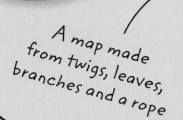

A map made from twigs, leaves, branches and a rope

2. Now walk in a straight line to another landmark, such as a building or waterfall, counting paces as you go. Work out how far you walked, using your pacing notes.

3. Work out a scale for your map. You might use 1 metre on the map to equal 100 metres in the real world. Then mark the landmark on your map, the correct distance and in the correct direction from your starting point.

Make a map from a hilltop

1. If you can find a good viewpoint, such as a hilltop, you can draw a map of the landscape around it. Mark the hilltop in the centre of a piece of paper. Then estimate the distance to other landmarks. Decide a scale for your map and mark landmarks in the correct directions. Add the scale and show which way is north by using a compass.

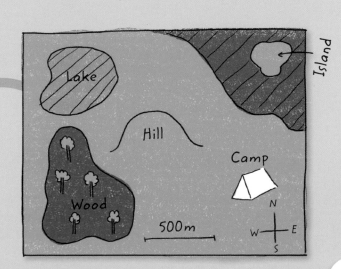

HUNT THE TREASURE!

TRY SOME GEOCACHING

Geocaching is an exploring game you can play with a GPS receiver. A GPS receiver tells you exactly where you are in the world, so you can find your position on a map. It will also guide you to landmarks. Geocaching is a good way to learn and practise GPS skills.

WHAT IS GPS?

GPS stands for Global Positioning System. A GPS receiver picks up signals from satellites and calculates its position in latitude and longitude. Some receivers are dedicated for navigation, but many mobile phones also do the job.

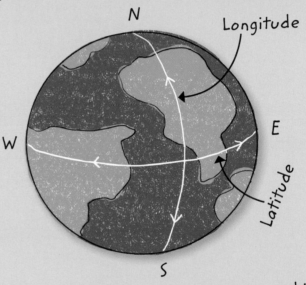

Your position is measured in latitude (the position north or south up and down the world) and longitude (the position east or west around the world). On a map, latitude goes up and longitude goes along.

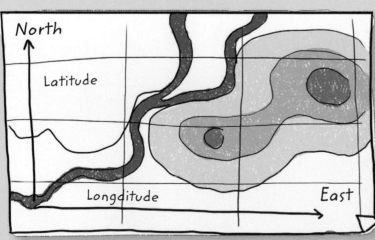

Leaving geocaches

1. Turn on your GPS unit (ask an adult to help you). Search for a good place to hide a prize, for example, between the branches of big tree. Put the prize in a plastic box to protect it. This is your first cache. Write a description of where the cache is, along with its latitude and longitude (from the GPS receiver).

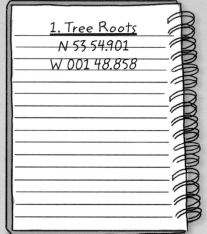

1. Tree Roots
N 53 54.901
W 001 48.858

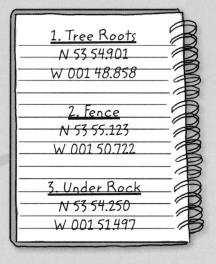

1. Tree Roots
N 53 54.901
W 001 48.858

2. Fence
N 53 55.123
W 001 50.722

3. Under Rock
N 53 54.250
W 001 51.497

Adding a waypoint to a GPS receiver

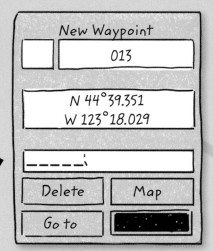

New Waypoint

013

N 44°39.351
W 123°18.029

_____

Delete   Map

Go to

2. Find some more hiding places for some more caches. Each time, write down a clue and the latitude and longitude.

3. Give your list to your friends. They must put the latitude and longitude of your caches into their GPS receivers. They can do this by creating waypoints and giving the waypoints a name.

Next Turn
Under the Rock

Time to Turn
00:01:57

Dist to Turn
00.49mi

A GPS receiver showing the way to a waypoint.

5. Following the arrow on a GPS takes you to the waypoint.

6. Make sure you collect up all your prizes at the end of the day.

4. Now your friends can ask their receivers to guide them to the caches, where they can find your prizes.

WILD ABOUT ROCKS

ROCKS, MINERALS, FOSSILS AND SHELLS

As you go exploring in the wild, you might climb rocks, throw rocks, skim rocks or trip over rocks! So why not add a magnifying glass to your rucksack, and have a look at the rocks you find? You might be lucky and find some amazing rock and mineral samples.

Identifying different rock types

ROCK TYPES

There are three types of rock:

- Igneous rocks are made when molten rock cools and becomes solid.

- Sedimentary rocks are made from layers of sand or silt.

- Metamorphic rocks are made when igneous or sedimentary rocks are changed by high temperature and immense pressure.

Crystals in a piece of granite, an igneous rock

1. If you can see obvious crystals in a piece of rock, it is probably igneous. You might need a magnifying glass to see the crystals. Igneous rocks are also dense and heavy.

Coloured bands in a piece of gneiss, a metamorphic rock

2. If the rock has grains running through it in bands or stripes, like crystals that have been flattened, melted and slightly mixed together, then it is probably metamorphic. These rocks are also very hard.

3. If the rock has a sandy, gritty feel, it is probably sedimentary. Sedimentary rocks are often quite soft and easy to break up.

Layers in a piece of sandstone, a sedimentary rock

4. You might see layers of sedimentary rocks that are folded and twisted.

Identifying common rocks

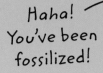

Haha! You've been fossilized!

Basalt

Limestone

Marble

Conglomerate

Schist

Identifying common minerals

Look at a piece of igneous rock, such as granite, to see the crystals of different minerals.

The minerals in granite:
feldspar (pink)
quartz (white)
biotite (black)

Escaping from lava

Volcanoes are great places to look at rocks, but what happens if a volcano erupts, and you are threatened by an eruption?

1. Lava bombs come flying through the air! Try to watch them as they fall, and dodge them as you run away.

2. You can normally outrun a lava flow. Don't climb a tree or shelter in a building, as lava will simply burn them to a crisp!

Run! Lava!

VOLCANO SAFETY

Never venture near a volcano without an expert guide

Searching for shells

You can find many different shells at the coast. They are the protective cases of sea creatures. You might find fossil shells, too.

1. Collect as many different shells as you can. Compare them to these common shells.

Razor shell

Cockle shell

Whelk shell

Mussel shell

Limpet shell

Searching for fossils

Fossils are the remains of plants and animals, that lived long ago, captured in rocks. If you find a fossil, you may be looking at the bones of an animal that lived millions of years ago!

1. You can find fossils where layers of some sedimentary rock are exposed, especially at the coast, and in the stones used for building, especially limestone and shale. Examine the rocks carefully. Break up the rocks into layers if you can, and look at flat faces.

FOSSIL FORMATION

Fossils are found in sedimentary rocks. They are formed when the remains of animals and plants get trapped in layers of sediment, which turn to rock over millions of years.

Ammonite

Crinoid

Shark tooth

Fern

Brachiopod

Doh!

2. Wash any mud off your fossils in a stream, then clean and dry them at home, and label them to show when and where you found them.

21

BIG SKIES

EXPLORING THE WEATHER

Out in the wild you are always aware of what the weather is like! Take some time to look up at the sky and you can learn a lot about how the weather works.

Should have checked the trees!

Cloud spotting

What sort of clouds can you see in the sky today? Clouds will help you to know what weather to expect.

Oh, look! A skunk!

Predicting rain

Some clouds warn of rain on the way. Look for cirrus clouds in a clear blue sky. They show that a weather front is approaching, so you can expect rain within a few hours.

Making a rain gauge

A rain gauge measures the amount of rain that falls.

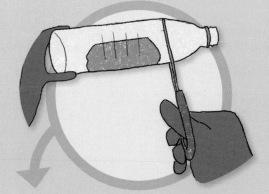

1. Cut off the top of a 2-litre plastic bottle.

2. Put a few stones in the bottom of the bottle, to stop it falling over, and add water to just above the curved base. Mark the water level with a pen. Put the top upside inside the bottom.

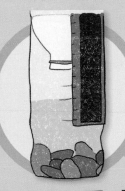

3. Put your rain gauge in the open, where rain can fall into it. At the same time each day, measure how much the water level has risen from the previous day, and record the result.

Weather clues

The prevailing wind is the direction from which the wind blows most often. Trees can show the direction of the prevailing wind.

1. Look at trees on hills to see if they are bent over. The way they bend shows which way the wind normally blows. Measure the direction the wind comes from with a compass.

TAKE COVER!

AVOIDING BAD WEATHER

Some weather, such as strong winds and lightning, can be deadly. So when you are exploring the wild, it's a good idea to know how to shelter when really bad weather is on the way.

Oops.

Predicting thunder and lightning

1. Always keep an eye on the sky when exploring the wild — it could save your life! If you see clouds with anvil-shaped tops (right), a thunderstorm could be on the way.

2. Count the number of seconds between seeing lightning and hearing thunder. This tells you how far away the storm is.

Cumulonimbus clouds bring thunder and lightning.

seconds	0	5	10	15	20	25	30

miles	0	1	2	3	4	5	6

kilometres	0	1	2	3	4	5	6	7	8	9	10

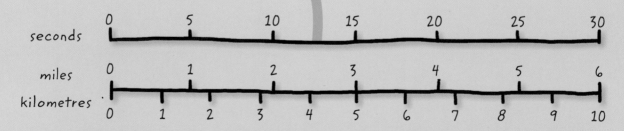

To measure the time between thunder and lightning, slide your finger along the top scale, then down to the bottom scale to see how far away the storm is.

Avoiding lightning in the wild

If a thunderstorm is getting closer, it's time for action...

1. If you can, go indoors, or get into a vehicle. Never shelter from heavy rain under a tree, or under an umbrella, as they will attract lightning.

Safe and unsafe places to shelter during a thunderstorm

The best place to sit in the mountains

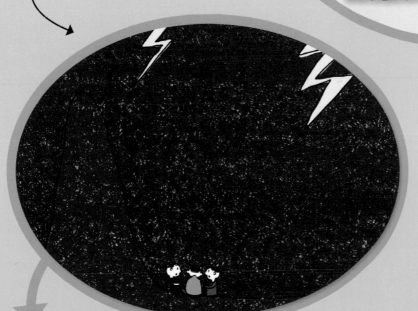

2. Lightning often strikes hilltops, so if you are on the summit of a hill, run downhill as fast as you can. Stay away from cliffs and caves, as lightning can flow down wet cliffs. Also keep away from open areas.

3. If you are caught out in the open, sit or crouch on your rucksack with your feet and hands off the ground.

STAR GAZING

NIGHT SKY WATCHING

At night in the wild, you often get a good view of the stars. That's because there are no street lights that make it hard to see them. A pair of binoculars will let you see more stars than you can with your naked eye.

Searching for constellations

Constellations are patterns made by stars in the night sky.

1. In the northern hemisphere, you should be able to find these constellations, depending on the time of year and the time of night:

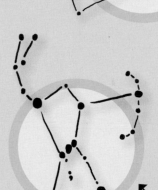

Pegasus (look for a big square of stars)

Ursa Major, aka the Plough or Big Dipper (like a giant pan)

Cassiopeia (like a huge M or W)

Orion (shaped like an egg-timer with a belt of bright stars)

2. In the southern hemisphere, you should be able to find these constellations, depending on the time of year and the time of night:

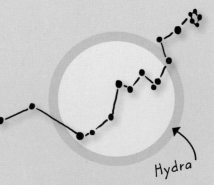

Hydra

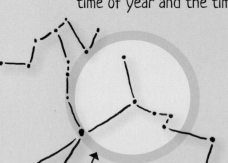

Centaurus

Crux, or the Southern Cross

3. In the southern hemisphere, you should also see two bright smudges of light. These are two galaxies called the Megallanic clouds.

Viewing the galaxy

The Milky Way is our galaxy, and is named after the bright band of light across the sky that you can see when it's very dark, as it is in the wild. The light comes from billions of stars.

Finding Polaris (the Pole Star) or the Southern Cross

You can navigate by the stars. Certain stars always point the way north or south.

North Star

1. In the northern hemisphere, look for the constellation of Ursa Major (right) Look along an imaginary line between the stars on the end of the pan to find a bright star. This is Polaris, the Pole or North Star.

2. In the southern hemisphere, find the Southern Cross (right). Next to the cross are two other bright stars. Imagine lines from the cross and these two stars. Where they meet is a point directly to the south.

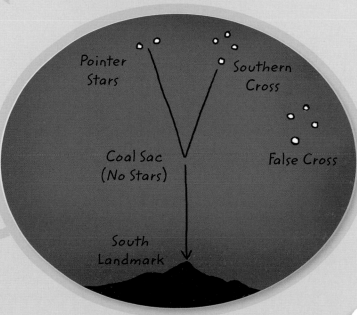

Pointer Stars

Southern Cross

Coal Sac (No Stars)

False Cross

South Landmark

Observing the Moon

The Moon is an amazing sight in the night sky. Some of its features are visible to the naked eye, but you can see lots of detail through a pair of binoculars. Look at the Moon on a clear night.

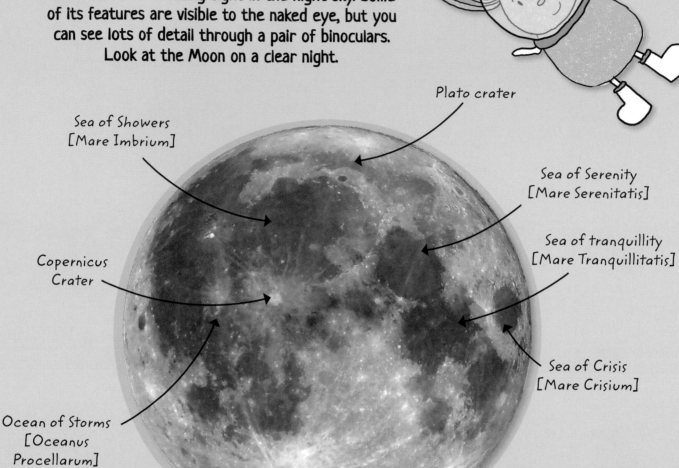

Plato crater

Sea of Showers [Mare Imbrium]

Sea of Serenity [Mare Serenitatis]

Sea of tranquillity [Mare Tranquillitatis]

Copernicus Crater

Sea of Crisis [Mare Crisium]

Ocean of Storms [Oceanus Procellarum]

Tycho Crater

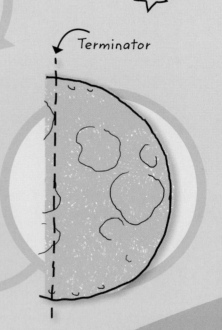

Terminator

1. The best way to look at the Moon is to sit in a chair or lie on your back, so you keep your head still. Look for light and dark areas. The dark areas are called seas, because the first astronomers thought they must be full of water. Can you identify the different seas? You might be able to see rays of dust fanning out from Tycho, a huge crater.

2. With binoculars you will be able to see dozens of craters, which you can identify with a proper Moon map. Look along the line between light and dark, called the terminator, on the Moon's surface to see detail in the craters. Put your binoculars on a tripod if you can.

Observing the Moon's phases

You must have seen the Moon's shape appear to change from one night to the next. Try recording these phases of the Moon.

1. Draw a series of circles on a sheet of paper. Look at the Moon at night and make a quick sketch of it inside the first circle. Repeat this each night. If you can't see the Moon, put an X through the circle.,

2. After a few days, you should see that the lit area of the Moon grows until it's full, then shrinks again.

Make sure you have some food, the moon isn't really made of cheese!

NORTH BY THE MOON

You can even find north or south by looking at the Moon! When the Moon is full, use the watch system on page 9, but point the hour hand at the Moon instead of the Sun.

DID YOU KNOW?

○ In 1804 the American explorers Meriwether Lewis and William Clark led an expedition to cross North America for the first time. It took them a year and a half to complete the 11,200 kilometre (7,000 mile) journey.

○ A compass needle always points to the magnetic north pole. This moves slowly around, at about 11 kilometres a year. At the moment it's in northern Canada.

○ Because of the difference between the position of the actual North Pole and the magnetic north pole, at the actual North Pole a compass needle always points south.

○ In some parts of the world, magnetic rocks under the ground affect compass needles, so compasses don't always point north.

○ Lodestone is a type of magnetic rock that contains lots of iron. The first compasses were made by dangling a piece of lodestone on a string. The lodestone always turned to face in the same direction.

○ Before GPS and other electronic navigation systems were invented in the 1960s, the only way to work out your position when far out at sea was to measure the exact position of the Sun and stars.

○ The first maps of the world didn't show North America, South America, Australia or Antarctica, as mapmakers didn't know these continents even existed.

Where have all the continents gone?!

O There's no evidence that pirate treasure maps ever existed! The idea of maps with a big X marking the location of buried treasure came from the story *Treasure Island*, written in 1883 by Robert Louis Stevenson.

O The geocaching craze was started for fun in the USA in 2000 by Dave Ulmer. There are now more than a million geocaches in the world, mainly in the USA.

O The first GPS system was developed in the 1960s by the US military. At first it was top secret, but now anyone can use it. The GPS receivers that the military use can work out their position to the nearest 30 centimetres (12 inches).

O The Earth was formed 4.5 billion years ago and the oldest fossils ever found are 3.5 billion years old. They are tiny microbes, and were discovered in Australia.

O The oldest rocks in the world are in Western Australia. They are 4.4 billion years old, and were formed when Earth was just 150 million years old.

O In 1977, lava from a volcano called Nyiragongo, in the Democratic Republic of Congo, flowed at speeds up to 60 kilometres per hour (40 miles per hour).

O With a good telescope you can see about 30,000 craters on the Moon, although there are thousands more that are too small to make out. The biggest crater, called Bailly, is 300 kilometres (186 miles) across.

INDEX

THE AUTHOR

Chris Oxlade is an experienced author of educational books for children. He has written more than two hundred books on science, technology, sports and hobbies, including many activity and project books. He enjoys camping and adventurous outdoor sports including rock climbing, hill running, kayaking and sailing. He lives in England with his wife, children, and dogs.

THE ARTIST

Eva Sassin is a freelance illustrator born and bred in London. She has loved illustrating ever since she can remember, and she loves combining characters with unusual textures to give them more depth and keep them interesting.